MEMORIES OF MUSIC FROM THE
1950s & 1960s

Pictures
to share

For May and Frank, who danced,
sang, and made memories to the
music from the 50's and 60's

**Pictures
to share**

Published in 2019 by
Pictures to Share Community Interest Company,
a UK based social enterprise that publishes
illustrated books for older people.

www.picturestoshare.co.uk

ISBN 978-0-9934049-4-8

Front Cover:
ELVIS PRESLEY, c. 1950s. Contributor: Everett Collection Inc / Alamy Stock Photo.

Front endpaper:
OCEAN'S ELEVEN Warner Bros 1960 film starring from l Peter Lawford, Dean Martin,
Sammy Davis Jnr and Frank Sinatra. Contributor: Pictorial Press Ltd / Alamy Stock Photo.

Rear endpaper:
Slipping A Disc - Mrs Batt inserting a record into the front of her in-car record player.
The music is fed into the car radio speaker system. Fox Photos / Getty Images.

Title page:
Dusty Springfield, Singer 1966. Contributor: AF Archive / Alamy Stock Photo.

MEMORIES OF MUSIC FROM THE 1950s & 1960s

Edited by Michelle Forster

This book can be enjoyed on its own or if you have access to the internet can be further enhanced and shared whilst listening to the songs on You Tube.

Let's rock everybody let's rock

Everybody in the whole cell block

Was dancin' to the Jailhouse Rock

JAILHOUSE ROCK, ELVIS PRESLEY, 1957

Contributor: Allstar Picture Library / Alamy Stock Photo.
Contributor: Pictorial Press Ltd / Alamy Stock Photo.
Contributor: Shawshots / Alamy Stock Photo.

The Top 10 biggest selling
Beatles songs:

1. She Loves You
2. I Want To Hold Your Hand
3. Can't Buy Me Love
4. I Feel Fine
5. Day Tripper/We Can Work It Out
6. Hey Jude
7. From Me To You
8. Help!
9. Hello Goodbye
10. Get Back

The Beatles

Portrait of the The Beatles. From left to right:
Ringo Starr, Paul McCartney, John Lennon, and George Harrison, circa 1965.

Bettmann / Contributor / Getty Images.

Que Sera Sera

When I was just a little girl
I asked my mother what will I be
Will I be pretty will I be rich
Here's what she said to me

Que Sera Sera
Whatever will be will be
The future's not ours to see
Que Sera Sera

What will be will be

Que Sera Sera by Doris Day

Mother and Daughter relaxing after cleaning.
Credit: Lambert / Getty Images.

Shirley Bassey was born in Cardiff in 1937. She had her first hit in 1957 with 'The Banana Boat Song'. Her most famous songs are:

'As I love you' – 1958

'Kiss Me Honey Honey Kiss Me' – 1959

'As Long As He Needs Me' -1960

'Reach For The Stars' – 1961

'I Who Have Nothing' – 1963

'Goldfinger' – 1964

'Big Spender' – 1967

SHIRLEY BASSEY Welsh singer.

Contributor: Pictorial Press Ltd / Alamy Stock Photo.

Pupils learn to twist in a dancing school, November 1961. A band in the United States had invented the dance and made it the most popular dance in the world by 1960. The Twist is basically a twisting motion back and forth with the hips

Contributor: dpa picture alliance / Alamy Stock Photo.

One two three o clock
four o clock rock

Five six seven o clock
eight o clock rock

Nine ten eleven o clock
twelve o clock rock

We're going to rock
around the clock tonight

ROCK AROUND THE CLOCK BILL HALEY

And His Comets

Burt Bacharach wrote songs for many artists including:

Magic Moments - Perry Como 1957

Baby It's You - The Shirelles 1961

Don't Make Me Over - Dionne Warwick 1962

Twenty Four Hours From Tulsa - Gene Pitaman 1963

Anyone Who Had a Heart - Dionne Warwick 1963

Walk on By - Dionne Warwick 1963

Trains, Boats and Planes - Burt Bacharach 1964

What's New Pussycat - Tom Jones 1965

Alfie - Cilla Black 1965

The Look of Love - Dusty Springfield 1967

I Say a Little Prayer - Dionne Warwick 1967

Raindrops Keep Falling on My Head - B J Thomas 1969

Burt Bacharach and Dionne Warwick recording a song at the
Pye studios in London. 1964.

Contributor: Trinity Mirror / Mirrorpix / Alamy Stock Photo.

THE VERY BEST OF
THE EVERLY BROTHERS

BYE BYE, LOVE • ('TIL) I KISSED YOU • WAKE UP, LITTLE SUSIE • CRYING IN THE RAIN • WALK RIGHT BACK • CATHY'S CLOWN • BIRD DOG • ALL I HAVE TO DO IS DREAM • DEVOTED TO YOU • LUCILLE • SO SAD • EBONY EYES

WB

WARNER BROS.
RECORDS
1554
newly recorded

© 1964, Warner Bros. Records Inc.

The Very Best of the
Everly Brothers album.

Contributor: CBW /
Alamy Stock Photo.

That'll Be
The Day

Peggy Sue

True Love Ways

Oh Boy

Everyday

Raining In
My Heart

Rave On

Buddy Holly And The Crickets.
Photo by John Rodgers / Redferns / Getty Images.

Johnny Cash's hits

Ring of Fire – 1963
I Walk The Line – 1956
Folsom Prison Blues – 1959
A Boy Named Sue – 1969

Hank Williams hits

I'm so Lonesome I Could Cry – 1949
Hey Good Lookin – 1951
You're Cheatin Heart – 1953

Patsy Cline hits

I Fall to Pieces – 1951
Walkin After Midnight – 1957
Crazy – 1961
Sweet Dreams – 1963

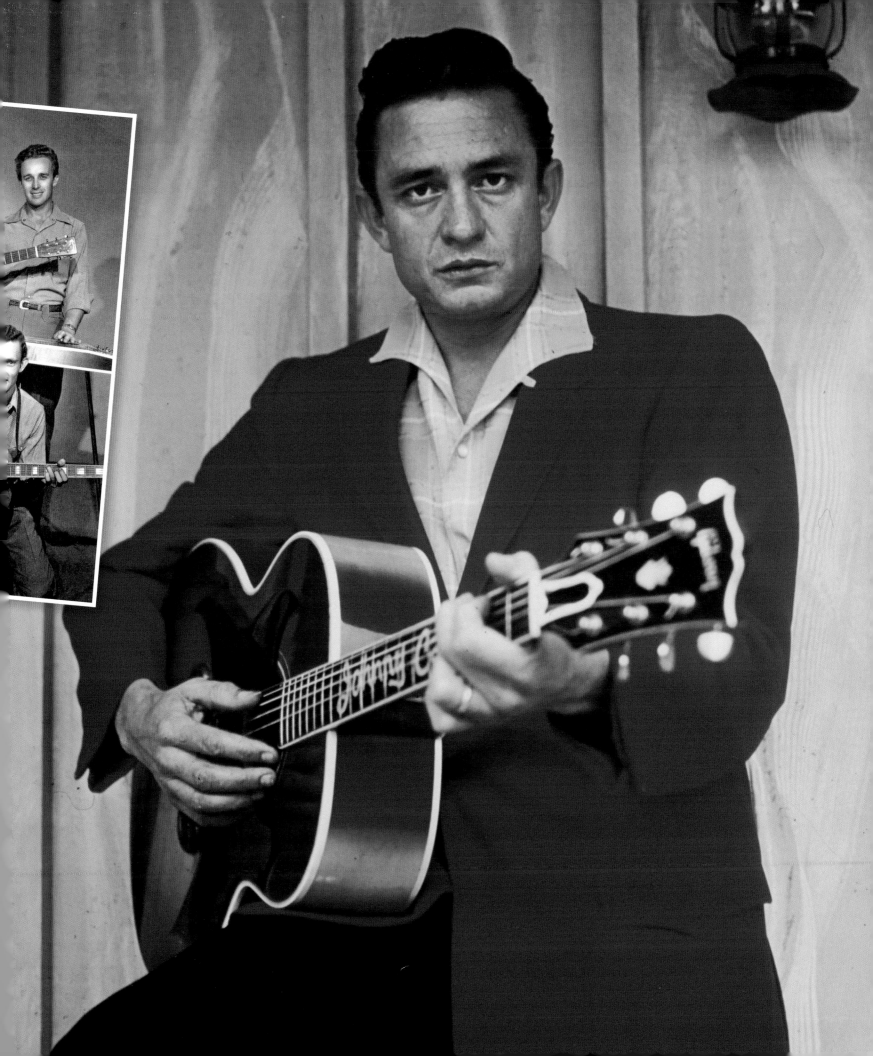

I'm Singing in the Rain

Gene Kelly, sings in the rain hanging on to a street lamp in the famous scene from the musical Singin' in the rain, 1952.

Photo by Mondadori Portfolio via Getty Images.

Catch a Falling Star

Catch a falling star and put it in your pocket
Never let it fade away
Catch a falling star and put it in your pocket
Save it for a rainy day

For love may come and tap you on the shoulder
some starless night
Just in case you feel you want to hold her
You'll have a pocketful of starlight

Catch a falling star and put it in your pocket
Never let it fade away
Catch a falling star and put it in your pocket
Save it for a rainy day

PERRY COMO (1912-2001) US singer 1965

Contributor: Pictorial Press Ltd / Alamy Stock.

The Hills are Alive with the Sound of Music

My Favourite Things

Sixteen Going on Seventeen

So Long Farewell

How do you Solve a Problem like Maria

Do Re Mi

Climb Every Mountain

Female Singers and Groups

Helen Shapiro
Walking back to Happiness 1962

Peggy March
I Will Follow 1963

The Angels
My Boyfriend's Back 1963

Cilla Black
You're My World 1964

Little Eva
The Locomotion 1962

Connie Francis
Who's Sorry Now 1958

The Ronettes
Be My Baby 1964

The Shangri-Las
The Leader of the Pack 1964

The Marvelettes
Please Mr Postman 1962

Mary Wells
My Guy 1964

The Supremes
Baby Love 1964

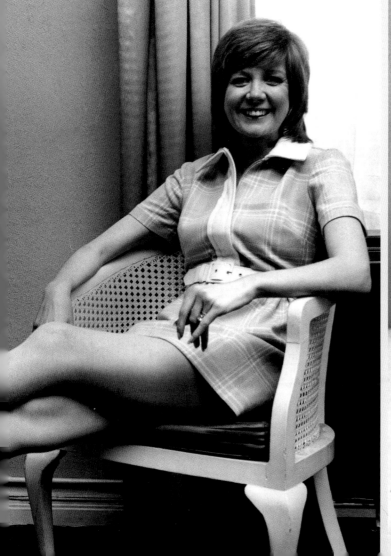

**Pictures
to share**

Graphic Design by Duncan Watts
Photo retouch by Studio 213

Published by
Pictures to Share
Community Interest Company.
Tattenhall, Cheshire
www.picturestoshare.co.uk

Printed in Europe through Beamreach Printing, Cheshire, UK

To see our other titles go to
www.picturestoshare.co.uk